FROM FLUNK OUT
TO FRONT OFFICE

by VaLarie Humphrey

Katie
Thanks
for support
Love

ISBN: 978-0-578-41254-2
Editors: P31 Publishing, LLC

For more information, please visit
www.valariehumphrey.com
Because of the dynamic nature of the Internet,
any web ad- dresses or links contained in this
book may have changed since publication and
may no longer be valid. The views expressed in
this work are solely those of the author and do
not necessarily reflect the views of the publisher,
and the publisher disclaims any responsibility
for them.
Any people depicted in stock imagery are
models, and such images are being used for
illustrative purposes only.

*Dedicated to the strongest two people
I have ever known, My parents,
Mr. & Mrs. Nathaniel Humphrey.
Your wisdom will play out through my
actions. It gives me strength to pursue
my purpose.*

CONTENTS

INTRODUCTION

Please don't judge me as I share my story. I didn't know any better. I didn't even know how to do better. Well, if you do judge me, it really doesn't matter at this point. I am so comfortable with the skin I'm in that I love me in spite of me. Just walk with me on this journey. Now let's get started.

You're reading a book written by a person who was flunked out of school but now runs a front office of a school. So when I tell you I flunked out, I FLUNKED OUT OF COLLEGE. I used to dress it up by saying cute stuff like, "I got invited to not return." That was one of my pretty ways of saying I FLUNKED OUT. When I became honest with myself, I had to change my language to reflect the God's honest truth which was simply that I FLUNKED OUT OF COLLEGE. Wow! It took me years to say that out loud and now it's on the cover of my book for the world to see.

It took me years to realize that I didn't listen to those around me with wisdom nor did I take heed to the warning signs. I simply thought that

I was supposed to live as the child I was mentally, and when the age of adulthood arrived, I would suddenly start living like it. Unbeknownst to the young me, I was supposed to prepare for adulthood. I just didn't know any better. Honestly, I really just didn't do any better.

FREEDOM AIN'T FREE

I was ready to go to college long before I actually left. I was ready to
be out of my parents' house and
"on my own." I was tired of listening
to them tell me what to do and when
to do it.

I used to say "I couldn't wait to BE
FREE." I walked around acting as if
someone owed me something. My
focus was not on college preparation
at all. It was on my friends and making

it around the neighborhood to party with everyone one last time. Sad to say, I had a ball. Again, I was WINNIN' AT LOSING.

It hadn't even crossed my mind that college was an extension of high school and that I needed to be even more responsible because no one would be there to keep me focused or reinforce those guidelines that would help me stay on the straight and narrow. I must have totally forgotten that I didn't graduate from high school on time. I still took graduation pictures and went to prom like everyone else in the Class of 1985.

The crazy thing was, I continued to live outside of my reality due to my lack of preparation in high school. I ended up attending the first college that accepted me. I was so excited to receive an acceptance letter that not once did I think that I wasn't ready. I planned out exactly what my dorm room was going to look like from the rugs to the walls. Even my towels had to be in line with my Garfield decor theme. I was so excited about shopping for all of my new, cute dorm stuff that it never really dawned on me that I wasn't truly socially or academically prepared to be successful in college.

I used to sit around talking crazy with my friend when my parents would make me angry. I could not wait to go to college to "BE FREE!" I was about to be free from my parents and all of "their rules." It was about to go down.

You see, I wanted to be able to go out when and where I wanted to, at any time. My mindset was disrespectful which caused my actions to not line up with the expectations that my parents had put in place. I used to sneak out of the house after they were asleep. Yup, me. I snuck out regularly! The crazy thing was, I used to sneak to drive around the town and sit on my friends' porches doing absolutely nothing. We would hang out until the wee hours of the morning. I would make it home right before dawn. I tell you, God had to be watching over me throughout my high school years. My male friends were my protectors more so than my biological brothers. My female friends were more like my sisters. We were one big happy family. Our theme song was "That's What Friends Are For."

Literally, I would wait for "the blow"... yep "the blow"...it went like this: beep beep - beep beep beep (1-2...1-2-3). Don't laugh! It meant grab your Levi jeans and let's roll out. Sad to say it truly meant, "time to ride out and sit around on someone's porch."

VaL Speaks Life

Freedom Ain't Free...I didn't realize that with freedom one must have discipline. That is one thing that I didn't have. As an adult I have had to develop discipline in all areas of my life. I actually became overweight because of my lack of discipline and overeating.

Discipline is one of those things that if you don't learn it while you're young, you will learn it the hard way later.

I didn't have discipline in my finances or my daily choices. My entire life ended up needing to be restructured to incorporate discipline strategies in all areas.

A VaL Nugget...

The lessons you learn because of the lack of discipline are ones that cost more than the price you would have paid the first time around.

WINNIN' @ LOSIN'

LOVE ME. Being able to say that didn't happen overnight. Actually, it took me 30 years. It took me 30 years to say it and actually believe it. You're reading this today because someone invested in you. I want you to get to the point where you understand what that means. When you say, "I love me," that means you will teach others how to treat you. The season in my life that I am about to share with you is not one of my proudest, but it is the one that grew me the most.

My GPA was 0.923 after first semester of college.. Please don't judge me. That was really my GPA! I used to be ashamed of it. A GPA less than 1, all the while I thought I was winning. You couldn't tell me anything back in the day.

Let's take a trip back in time briefly to my high school days. I was a member of the Class of 1985 at Proviso West High School in Hillside, Illinois. Yes, 1985! Please believe that I am still cute. Graduation day was full of a lots of the traditional pomp and circumstance, family fun and celebrations. Y'all know the traditional graduation song right? (duuun nunna nuh nuuun nuh...LOL) Most people call it the Graduation Song. For future reference, it's titled "Pomp and Circumstance", but I still call it the Graduation Song.

If y'all were anything like me, you also couldn't wait for the moment. Just to hear that song and put on my cap and gown. I envisioned myself strolling into the gym with my head held high, as my grandma and family would be looking on proudly. My parents would be ready to record the whole thing, my mother was going to be crying the whole time because her baby girl was about to walk across the stage and get her high school diploma. You see, where I'm from, the whole entire family attends a family member's graduation.

I realize that some of you will have to think back a little bit further than others to remember your graduation day. I was so geeked up sitting in the parking lot in a car hanging out with my friends while my classmates were on their way into the graduation ceremony, I WAS STILL WINNING!

We were WINNING, so I thought. We were having a ball. Sitting in the car talking about the other students' parents and grandparents. We were cracking up. I was not able to walk across the stage because I flunked

English class my senior year in high school. Now everyone knows you cannot fail a class your senior year. I didn't get that at the time, because again, I was WINNING. I believed it was okay, because I knew all of the answers to the wrong questions. Sad to say, I just didn't get it.

VaL Speaks Life

I really thought I was experiencing success and heading in the right direction.. We were literally in the parking lot at the Proviso West High School, watching people walk in. This is my truth. This is a true manifestation of my mindset in high school. I had to finish up in summer school. That same mindset unfortunately went to college with me.

It took me a minute to realize that I was WINNING AND LOSING at the same time. Truth be told, I was WINNING AT LOSING. I kept hanging out with the same types of people who shared that delusional mindset. I am loyal so I held on to my old friends and did the same old things.

I never asked my WINNIN' friends what they wanted to be when they grew up. Never thought about having the conversation, not even what college they wanted to go to. Didn't even ask what their GPA was. I should have asked if their GPA looked like mine. We didn't have those conversations, because all I thought about was who dressed nicely, so we should be friends. I did not realize that friends should help one another accomplish their dreams and goals, EVEN IN HIGH SCHOOL. I attended the first college that accepted me.

Here is the rest of my truth...I flunked out of college after my first year because I didn't realize that I was privileged. I didn't realize that going to school was a privilege, being in a household with two parents was a privilege. Everyone who was telling me to change what I was doing, wasn't crazy. Everyone who was telling me to dress a little differently, they were not crazy.

A VaL Nugget...

If two or more people who are not connected to one another tell you, suggest to you, or down right demand that you change something about you, WITHOUT HESITATION, YOU BETTER BEGIN THE TRANSFORMATION.

BOARD OF DIRECTIONS

Second day at college and I am as free as a butterfly. I walked across campus and back. I hung out all day. I stopped by a few barbeques and went shopping for some odds and ends. When I arrived back at the dorm, my ENTIRE floor was empty. I went knocking on doors up and down the hall. No one answered. The floor was completely quiet. I went back into my room for about an hour and finally I heard folks getting off of the elevator. I jumped up and ran out in the hallway. "Hey y'all! Where y'all been?" Well low and behold, the entire floor was in a mandatory meeting that took place in the lounge on a different floor.

Right in middle of me trying to get the details, around the corner comes the RA. The RA, resident assistant, is a trained peer leader who supervises the dorm residents. They are basically the managers of the entire floor. Seeing that we were all freshmen and really had no clue about how to be successful in college, we were asked to attend a mandatory meeting. Soon after the RA turned the corner she began to walk straight towards me. I felt like I was in third grade at Wilson Elementary and Mrs. Biggs called my name for my homework and I did not have it.

She began to walk towards my desk to hear my lame excuse as to why I did not have it. Talking about wanting to run and hide. That feeling came back and again I had no clue what to do. My feet were nailed to the floor. What was actually three to five seconds seemed like an hour and a half! I seriously panicked. With a stern voice she said, "Are your VaLarie Humphrey from room 1616?" Softly and slowly I said, "Yes, I am." Ready to give MY valid excuse as to why I wasn't at the MANDATORY meeting. She said, "Did you not read the announcement on the bulletin board in reference to the meeting?" I turned and looked at the huge bulletin board that you can't miss when you get off of the elevator. I read it and then felt about as small as I used to after giving Mrs. Biggs my GREAT excuse for not having my homework. I didn't even try to explain myself. All I could do at that point was walk over and read all of the announcements on the HUGE bulletin board.

VaL Speaks Life

I never wanted to feel that way again. Especially not in front of my college peers. From that day forward as I exited the elevator I walked over to the HUGE bulletin board and read all of the flyers and actually wrote the event details down.

This story illustrates the simplest principle in my book. All I can say is JUST READ THE BULLETIN BOARDS. Back in my day, it was bulletin boards and flyers. Now a days it's emails and websites. It is up to you to stay informed and act accordingly.

This was one of the major lessons I learned in college in a pretty elementary way. It meant so much more than just read the bulletin board. It was a lesson on being aware of my surroundings and don't take the little things for granted. You see, the board didn't scream READ ME nor was I told that it was a task to do daily. It was one of those subtle things that most people just assume you would do. Later, I found out that the information shared during that meeting was about surviving life in the dorms and avoiding the unnecessary pitfalls that most freshmen fall into.

The only way to function on a level of excellence is to definitely grab the low hanging fruit. Ok, what the heck is "low hanging fruit?" It's those easy things to take care of that may or may not take up a lot of your time. The term "grab the low-hanging fruit" is a frequently used metaphor for doing the simplest or easiest thing first or for a quick fix that produces results, quickly. As my mentor always says, "small wins make big dreams come true." Taking care of small wins first will allow you to experience the feeling of success while working towards a bigger goal...that BIG DREAM. Those small wins will help you move faster towards your goals and dreams with confidence. Now go grab some low hanging fruit and eat up!

A VaL Nugget...

Once again, small wins make big dreams come true! Inch by inch to make a foot.

DISTRACTIONS

In college my distractions took over my life. It became apparent that I allowed my distractions to be more powerful than my decisions. Allow me to walk you through what that looked like for me.

I am going to share my experience with a student who volunteered during a group workshop session, I will refer to as Taylor.

Val: "Thank you for volunteering. So what's your name?"

Taylor: "Taylor."

VaL: "Hi, Taylor. How are you?"

Taylor: "Good. How are you?"

VaL: "I'm amaaazing! My name is Ms. VaL. I'm gonna give you a goal. Your goal is to go to that door. Please tell me what your goal is?

Taylor: "To go to that door."

VaL: Okay. Tell me your goal.

Taylor: My goal is to go to that door.

VaL: Okay, cool. (I asked the audience) What's her goal?

Audience: "To go to the door."

VaL: "Cool. Now what year are you in school Taylor?"

Taylor: "2020. (Blank stare from me because I had not clue what year in school she was.) A Junior now."

VaL: "Oh a junior, oh wow, I'm a proud member of the Class of 1985, that's all I know. You said, "2020", I was so lost. I am with you now. So how many siblings do you have?

Taylor: None. I'm an only child.

VaL: What elementary school did you attend?

I continued to ask arbitrary questions. People in the audience began to whisper. The whispers got louder and louder. Some people began to get a tad bit frustrated. All of a sudden someone yelled, "Girl! Get to the door! You getting off track, she is distracting you!"

Taylor: "OMG, you were distracting me, that's not fair!" (She then took off running toward the door and the crowd began the cheer her on.)

I looked at the audience and laughed with pure joy.

VaL Speaks Life

At first, the audience was in, they were listening to the answers that Taylor was sharing. They were listening intently. They were all in with the sound effect you hear when people think something is cute. Just like I was distracting her with pleasurable conversation, I was asking all about her. That is what will happen in life because some distractions are pleasurable.

That is exactly what happened to me my freshman year in college. I arrived on campus and began to take interest in all of the things that were truly distractions. I was so distracted from the purpose of why I was in college that by the time I realized what was going on, I had already flunked out of college.

AGAIN, distractions can be pleasurable. When distractions

come, they are going to be enticing and engage you. So here is the breakdown:

- The folks who were angry, were angry because they heard her goal and wanted to hold her accountable. (a keeper)

- To some, she was a fish in a bowl and they just watched as she became more and more distracted. Some friends will watch you make mistakes and say nothing. (a throw away... not truly really worth keeping)

- Some folks began to question her about her choice to stand there and chat with me. Some people will ask you about that goal you shared with them and begin to question how your current actions are aligned with the goal that you shared. (a keeper)

When keepers come into your life, they will hold you accountable for your own dreams.

Now think about it, I never told anyone to hold her accountable for her goal. But when you tell people, "When I grow up I want to be a teacher", true friends will call you out because they see that your actions are not aligned with your goals. That includes calling you out even when you don't agree with what they are telling you.

Self-assessment needs to happen at all times.

A VaL Nugget...

when you make mistakes or get off track, watch and listen to how your inner team responds. You may need to do some trading of team members.

MY MOTHER'S VOICE

Who knew that actually getting all the freedom I wanted would almost cost me me. The crazy thing is that I lost myself in all of the freedom. I wasn't going to class, I wasn't cleaning my room and I wasn't focused on the true purpose of why I was in college.

While sitting on the side of my bed in my dorm room I began to see my life spiraling out of control. To be honest, I was scared out of my mind. At this point I was beginning to wonder how to pull it all back together. I looked around my room at the clothes everywhere and dishes on my desk- that desk that I never used for studying. I just shook my head and then all of a sudden I began to hear my mother's voice, "Why are you living like this? Look at your room. Look at your life." I began to answer those questions with excuses as to why my life was in shambles.

It didn't take long before I began to straighten up my room and pull myself together. The sad thing was that it was too late to actually pull my grades up before the end of the semester. I had no real clue what to do. I did it again, went on with the winnin' at losin' mindset and decided to ride it out. I continued down the path of destruction, but with a clean room.

VaL Speaks Life

I really didn't stop. I can't even begin to tell you why. Allow me to share the crazy part of this; my friends were going to class. I was sleeping all day hanging out with them at night. I missed the mark. I was so focused on one thing I missed the real thing. THEY WERE GOING TO CLASS.

VaL Nugget

...after self assessing, make the changes so things will change.

BROKEN CRAYONS
STILL COLOR

I wouldn't really call it a comeback because I never stopped grinding after flunking out of college. I entered into a true grind season. That day in May of 1986 that I opened my report card and saw the words "ACA-DEMIC SUSPENSION", my world shattered. After getting over feeling sorry for myself I began to problem-solve how to get my life back together.

I enrolled into Jr College trying to get my grades back up so I could get back into Western Illinois University. Every day I had to take the bus, the train and then walked eight blocks to get to class. Ain't no way to prettily walk eight blocks. Winter, spring, summer, and fall, I had to do this for a year. I envisioned myself graduating and walking across Western Illinois University's stage. Remember, I didn't walk across the stage in high school. So I had to pull that back together.

So once I regrouped, I refocused. When I tell you I refocused, I had to set some goals. I had to keep my eyes on the prize. I had to keep going reminding myself of what I wanted.

So when I got back into Western, I moved to the other side of campus, I had to stop playing. I learned the hard way that there was no recess in college. I couldn't hang out with those same WINNING people. I actually moved on to a 24 hour quiet floor. That meant you were expected to be completely quiet 24 hours a day...and I seriously needed to shut up and get my life together. I did way too much talking my freshman year. So when I got back, I learned to shut up and take action. I moved to the other side of the campus, a major thing I learned was not to live with my friends. I didn't have to live in the middle of the party to enjoy college life.

See, I was that one, "Val, turn the lights out so the party can start. (5 hours later) Val, turn the lights back on because everybody has to go home!" I was there from the beginning to the end of all of the parties.

I didn't think there was a problem with that. I didn't, because I was WINNING. Again, I was WINNING at losing. I didn't get it.

So, what happened? I developed grit. That bounce-back, that endurance to accomplish a goal that I had set, because I now wanted to graduate. Not walking across the stage in high school began to haunt me. I still went to prom like I was going to graduate on time. I looked so pretty on prom, yet I wasn't graduating.

I never walked across the high school stage. I became ashamed for a long time, but when I was WINNING at losing, I wasn't ashamed. I did so much to cover it up, I was the cool girl on campus. It was like putting a broken gift in a pretty box and putting a bow on it, that's exactly what I did too. I figured out how to wrap it so it would look cute on the outside and others would think I was cute on the inside.

VaL Speaks Life

Some of us are wrapped up all pretty and trying to hide that we're broken. I opened up to my truth, I just shouted it out to the world "MY GPA AFTER MY FIRST YEAR IN COLLEGE WAS A 0.923!" It took me a minute to truly embrace my past and start living my best life ever. My journey now is so much more impactful to the world and those that I encounter on a daily basis.

It took a whole lot of truth for me to find freedom. If you didn't know it by now then let me tell you, I LOVE ME, THE PAST ME AND THE CURRENT ME. HECK, I AM ALREADY IN LOVE WITH THE FUTURE ME. I cannot wait to meet her. In July of 1995 I became an Assistant Principal at a middle school in Aurora, Illinois. Yep, from a college FLUNK OUT TO THE FRONT OFFICE of a school.

It took me almost 20 years to realize that I was broken, then another 10 to realize that a BROKEN CRAYON STILL COLORS. I have been coloring true masterpieces with the brokenness of my past. I was once broken and thought I had no value. I thought that I would never find my purpose in life. Well, well, well, from that dropout came a true masterpiece. Rarely do people even talk about me flunking out anymore-heck, they don't even believe me. LOL, I am usually the one bringing it up. Look at the back cover and know it can be done.

A VaL Nugget...

Turn your weakness into a strength and you will develop grit as you grind through this thing called life. It's a life sentence, so you might as well live it to the fullest.

DON'T EAT IN THE TEACHER'S LOUNGE

After graduating from college I was so excited to begin my teaching career. I went to the woman that I watched teach and impact the lives of children for many years, my beloved Mother. I went to her to ask for some teacher advice. I waited for her words of wisdom with full anticipation and she looked at me and said, "Don't eat in the teachers' lounge," then turned to continue about her business. I stood there with a blank look on my face waiting to hear more. Nothing came. I thought to myself, really? That's all you got? You've been teaching 30 som'n years and all you come with is "Don't eat in the teachers' lounge!" All I could think was, alright Mother, I won't eat in the teachers' lounge. Cool, I got it!

So my first five years of teaching I was avoiding the teacher's lounge like there was a plague in there or something. Those days and times that I was invited to eat in the teachers' lounge by my co-workers and friends (like breathing), I would smile and quickly say, "No thank you, I can't eat in the teacher's lounge." I began to invite my coworkers and friends into my room to have lunch with me. Several of them actually joined me and then one day, it hit me like a ton of bricks. It took me five years to realize what my mother truly meant. She wasn't talking about eating my food in the teacher's lounge. A huge smile appeared on my face and I began to laugh out loud and say... "DON'T EAAAAT IN THE TEACHERS' LOUNGE! WOW! MOTHER REALLY!" People around me thought I was crazy because my mother was nowhere near, not even in a 5 mile radius. I then said out loud, "She was talking about feeding off of the negative energy in the teacher's lounge, not my lunch. All I could do was laugh and clap my hands. Maybe you don't know it, but the teachers' lounge is not just a place where teachers are known for just eating their food, it's also the place where some teachers share their negative experiences about their daily encounters with students, parents, other co-workers and let's not leave out administration. I finally understood and after 28 years, I still don't eat in the teachers' lounge, thanks to the amazing advice from my dear mother.

VaL Speaks Life

You won't always understand nuggets of wisdom when they are

shared with you. The best thing you can do is abide by them until clarity comes. Like me, it may take years, but continue to apply the wisdom and it'll pay off. I have avoided the negativity that brewed in the teachers' lounges in every school that I have worked at. After over twenty-eight years, my connections and positive daily outlook on life continue to grow and allow me to love the life I live.

Your circle of influence, when it comes to your friends, is the most important to pay attention to. Those closest to you will influence the majority of your decisions. That is usually where you go for advice. Know your immediate circle better than you know yourself. Friends that don't hold you accountable for getting to your dreams and goals should be cut off. I am clear that it sounds harsh, but cutting them off will allow you to grow faster and go further. Peer pressure can be a good thing when it is positive.

A VaL Nugget...

Eagles can get low like chickens, but just know, the chickens can't get high like the eagles. So make the conscious decision to soar.

THE KIDNEY STORY...
LOOK INSIDE FIRST

September 2008 I was sitting in the doctors office waiting for him to come in. I was so excited that my mother was with me because we were having a girls' shopping day. After a few long minutes, the doctor came in and finished my physical so fast. Before walking out he looked at my mother and said, "You haven't had blood work or a physical in a while, let's send you for blood work today then follow up next week with a physical." Without a care we went down to the lab and then went shopping.

Her follow up appointment was a week later. We were sitting in the office and the wait time felt like an eternity. After what seemed like a lifetime, the doctor came in with a stoic look on his face. The conversation began with, "Mrs. Humphrey I recommend you see a specialist. Your kidney function blood work came back alarming. I strongly recommend you see a nephrologist as soon as possible." Talking about a shocker and nail biter.

A boat load of blood work and an appointment later we were hit with the heart wrenching news that my mother's kidney function was at 14%. Talking about questions and confusion...oooooweeee! After three years of doctor appointments and continuous trips to the lab for blood work, we were hit again with sobering news. Now my mother's kidney function was under 5%. The situation got REAL real fast. After three years, it was time to make some serious decisions.

Her kidneys' function was decreasing really fast. They had basically stopped functioning. Initially, she refused to have dialysis and refused to have a kidney transplant. She finally tried dialysis and after a while, we were told that dialysis wasn't working. The first thought that came to mind was, "Oh no, she can't die." My mother finally agreed to try for a kidney transplant. On June 19, 2012 we all (my three brothers, my mom and I) went in for a transplant consultation meeting.

We went through the meeting and the nurse looked at us, the children, and asked the big question, "Are you all willing to donate?" Without a moment of hesitation we all agreed to be tested. They began handing out documents for us to sign to agree to the testing. The first statement following handing out the documents was, "If you have high blood pressure you are not able to donate." Unfortunately, my brothers all have high blood pressure and did not qualify to be tested to donate a kidney to our mother. I, on the other hand, did not have high blood pressure or anything else going on that would initially prevent me from being tested.

My three brothers gave back their forms. I was the first and only person tested, they took seventeen vials of blood that day. Seventeen vials of blood and 2 hours later, they called me and with the exciting news that I was a qualified match so far. I was asked to return back the next day. The testing began that day and did not stop for thirty-eight days...July 26, 2012. They needed to do my workup first. They were running all of these tests and one of the test was an HIV/AIDs test. I was 45 at the time. Needless to say I was a tad bit nervous.

While waiting the 24 hours for the test results, all I can say is that that was the longest 24 hours of my life. All night, I sat up thinking about all of the choices that I made during my 45 years that may impact me being able to save my mother's life. Every decision that I made earlier in my life to have unprotected sex could now impact my ability to give my mother another chance at life. Knowing that I didn't even have that many sexual partners, I was still nervous.Could I have AIDS? I wondered. That one test could stop me from giving my mother a kidney, knowing I was a strong match was petrifying. WOW, because of a choice I made when I was younger, my mother could die. That was a looooong 24 hours.

I arrived at the hospital early the next day to get my results. Waiting with a true level of nervousness, and a desire for God to give me some do overs. The nurse came in, it was like she was walking so slowly and then she started talking slow too. She started sharing the results of all of the other test..I promise, I didn't care. All I could think was, DO I HAVE AIDS? IS MY MOTHER GOING TO DIE BECAUSE OF A CHOICE I MADE EARLIER IN MY LIFE?

I am not going to make you wait until the end of the book to find out...

VaL Speaks Life

Just know that this is a true story! This was one of the hardest days of my life. All I could think about was those times where I thought I was in love so I didn't protect myself. I began to realize that a decision I made when I was a teen could stop me from saving my mother's life. That tore me up inside for 24 hours.

I don't understand why we struggle so much with making a decision to save our own lives when it could possibly save someone else's life as well. On July 26, 2012, I gave my mother a kidney. She lived 6 additional years. #10-4 Good Buddy (that's our love language we never said, "Goodbye" to one another, we always said, "10-4")

A VaL Nugget...

Two nuggets here with this story:

- You have everything you need right there inside of you, even when you feel like you have nothing and nowhere to go. All those doctor visits and I had the kidney right there inside of me the whole time.

- Make smart, sound decisions today because you are becoming someone's lifesaver tomorrow.

TWIGS BUILD STRONG NESTS

If you know me then you have already heard about my foundation. If you have not, then let me share a little about it. My foundation is called True Eagle Beauty Foundation, Incorporated, because an eagle is an amazing bird.

It's truly a beautiful story, let's say.

The first amazing thing about them is that they mate for life, no joke. They really do. There is a specific type of female eagle out there that will put a male eagle through a little test before mating with him.

The female eagle will pick up a twig, a branch, a part of the tree, and fly as high as 61 football fields, that's 21,960 feet. The male eagle follows her as she soars higher and higher. She drops the twig and looks at the male... "CATCH IT, BEFORE IT HITS THE GROUND."

He then swoops down and grabs the twig before it hits the ground. He then brings the twig back to her. She then flies even higher, and drops it again and once again looks at him again... "CATCH IT BEFORE IT HITS

THE GROUND." Again, he swoops down and grabs the twig again. At any point, if he lets the twig hit the ground, she will not mate with him. Yep, deuces, kick rocks, be gone! She does this for a minimum of two hours, soaring higher and higher each time. Yeah, the guy has to catch it before it hits the ground and bring it back every single time. I already know the looks on the guys' faces. The guys are thinking, SHE MUST BE OUT OF HER MIND, I AM NOT DOING THAT! If he continues to catch the twig THEN AND ONLY THEN will she mate with him.

After this 2 hour dance in the air, she will mate with him, if he hasn't allowed the twig to hit the ground, of course.

They then have baby eagles that are called eaglets.

Now, when it's time to teach the eaglets to fly, well shall I say soar, the mother eagle pushes them out of the nest and immediately looks at papa eagle..."CATCH MY BABY... BEFORE HE HITS THE GROUND." He immediately begins to go down with the baby eagle attempting to show him how to stretch out its wings so it can soar. Right before the eaglet is about to hit the ground, papa eagle swoops in and grabs the eaglet and takes it back to the nest. This continues for a minimum for two hours. So she keeps pushing, and he keeps catching.

PAUSE RIGHT HERE...YOU GET WHY SHE TESTED HIM WITH THE TWIG?

VaL Speaks Life

Let's go back...She knew from the beginning that he was going to catch her baby, because she tested him with that twig. Did you get that? She knew he wasn't going to be her "baby daddy", he wasn't going to be a deadbeat dad, and he wasn't going to leave no matter how hard it got, no matter how long it took to get this baby to soar. Whatever it took! She knew from the get go, that she wasn't going to be a single baby momma. How did she know? I'm glad you asked. She knew it because she tested him before she trusted him. To us, it was a branch, a twig, a piece of a tree that she used to test him. What she did was find out if he would be there to catch a twig to give her the security of knowing he would catch their baby.

A VaL Nugget...

... So if God, gave that much sense to a bird, why don't we test before we trust? Really? What does testing a person look like compared to a twig? Now what you choose to do with that information is up to you. Once the twig has hit the ground, will you be willing to walk away? So with that said, TEST BEFORE YOU TRUST. DROP A TWIG OR TWO.

I FINALLY WOKE UP

As an adult I look back and truly wonder why I made some of the decisions I made. I must admit, I wouldn't do EVERYTHING over again if I had the chance. I must admit I am who I am because of the decisions made. Knowing life could have been a little bit sweeter makes me feel a little disappointed...just a little.

The day I agreed to actually change was the day my life began to change.

As long as I wasn't really willing to try to change, nothing changed. The hardest struggle was actually making that same decision to change everyday. While on this journey called life I learned to self- assess regularly along the way. I now assess my friends, my family, my decisions and most of all the use of my time.

My life got so much easier when I actually began to set goals and focus on them. I began to write down my short and long term goals and share them.

I can feel the smile from my parents in heaven. Every now and then I can tell that God is winking at me.